HOW TO MASTER YOUR FOCUS

Increase Productivity, Sustain Growth and Development, Improve Self-Confidence, and Build Success Mindset to Grow Fast.

PRADIP DAS

© Copyright 2024 - All rights reserved.

The content contained within this book may not be reproduced, duplicated, or transmitted without direct written permission from the author or the publisher. Under no circumstances will any blame or legal responsibility be held against the publisher, or author, for any damages, reparation, or monetary loss due to the information contained within this book. Either directly or indirectly.

Legal Notice:
This book is copyright protected. This book is only for personal use. You cannot amend, distribute, sell, use, quote or paraphrase any part, or the content within this book, without the consent of the author or publisher.

Disclaimer Notice:
Please note the information contained within this document is for educational and entertainment purposes only. All effort has been executed to present accurate, up to date, and reliable, complete information. No warranties of any kind are declared or

implied. Readers acknowledge that the author is not engaging in the rendering of legal, financial, medical or professional advice. The content within this book has been derived from various sources. Please consult a licensed professional before attempting any techniques outlined in this book.

By reading this document, the reader agrees that under no circumstances is the author responsible for any losses, direct or indirect, which are incurred as a result of the use of information contained within this document, including, but not limited to, — errors, omissions, or inaccuracies.

Please scan for the other book of the series
"Life Mastery".

Table of Contents

Table of Contents 4
Introduction 5
Decoding The Art of Focus 8
Crafting Crystal-Clear Goals................... 23
Distraction-Free Living............................ 31
Enhancing Concentration Sharpness . 39
Maximizing Efficiency and Output....... 55
Building Unbreakable Mental Strength
 64
Designing Your Perfect Workspace 71
Taking Control of Your Thoughts 85
Final Thoughts 96

Introduction

In the exciting world of chess, where every move is like a carefully planned puzzle piece, a new group of young Indian chess players is making big waves worldwide. Think of talented youngsters like D Gukesh and Praggnanandhaa, who started from humble beginnings, playing in small tournaments all over India. Now, in just a few years, they've become famous worldwide for their incredible skills.

These young players have worked incredibly hard and beaten some of the best chess players globally. They've climbed up the ranks and are now among the top 20 players in the world. And they've done all this while still being very young.

Their story is truly inspiring because it demonstrates that with laser focus and dedicated practice, anyone can turn their dreams into reality. They've become heroes for young chess fans everywhere, showing that age is no barrier to achieving greatness. As they continue to play, they're teaching us that there are no limits to what we can achieve if we work hard and persevere.

As we wonder at their meteoric rise to fame, we are reminded of the importance of honing our own powers of concentration in pursuit of our goals. Whether we're striving for success in our careers, seeking personal fulfillment, or simply navigating the complexities of everyday life, the lessons of focus imparted by these young chess maestros are invaluable.

In this book, we will go into the details of the secrets of mastering focus, drawing inspiration from the extraordinary journeys of Gukesh, Pragganandhaa and many other world class chess players. Through their stories, we will uncover practical strategies and techniques for sharpening our concentration, eliminating distractions, and achieving our highest aspirations.

Decoding The Art of Focus

Focus is like a superpower that allows us to direct our attention and energy towards a specific task or goal. It's what enables us to block out distractions, hone in on what matters most, and perform at our best, whether we're on the playing field, in the classroom, or at work.

Defining Focus and Its Significance:

At its core, focus is about being fully present and engaged in the moment, channeling all our mental and physical resources towards a singular objective. It's what separates the great from the good, the champions from the contenders.

But focus isn't just reserved for elite sportsman and business tycoons – it's a skill that anyone can cultivate and harness to achieve their goals. Whether you're studying for an exam, working on a project, or pursuing a passion, cultivating focus can help you perform at your best and make meaningful progress towards your objectives.

In today's world, where distractions abound and our attention is constantly pulled in a million different directions, mastering focus has never been more important. By understanding the true meaning of focus and its significance in achieving success, we can unlock our full potential and accomplish remarkable feats in our own lives. So, let's embrace the power of focus and unleash our inner champions, one focused moment at a time.

Focus is like a mental spotlight that allows us to direct our attention towards specific tasks, thoughts, or sensations while filtering out distractions. It's what enables us to concentrate on what matters most and tune out the noise around us. But focus isn't just about paying attention – it's also about being fully present and engaged in the moment, whether we're studying for an exam, practicing a skill, or having a conversation with a friend.

Different Types of Focus

Task-Oriented Focus: This type of focus involves directing our attention towards completing a specific task or achieving a particular goal.

Creative Focus: Creative focus involves immersing ourselves in a creative endeavor, whether it's writing, painting, or composing music.

Social Focus: Social focus involves being fully present and attentive in social interactions, whether with family, friends, or colleagues.

Strategic Focus: Strategic focus involves zooming out to see the bigger picture and planning for the future.

Mindfulness Focus: Mindfulness focus involves cultivating awareness of our thoughts, feelings, and sensations in the present moment.

Understanding the different types of focus can help us harness our mental powers more effectively and achieve our goals with greater clarity and purpose. Whether we're striving for professional success, pursuing creative endeavors, or nurturing relationships, cultivating the right kind of focus can make all the difference in our journey towards success and fulfillment.

The Science of Focus

In present scenario, the ability to focus has become more crucial than ever. But what exactly is focus, and how does our brain process it?

Have you ever wondered how our brains manage to stay focused amidst the noise and distractions of the world around us? Let's take a closer look at how the brain processes focus, using the example of world-class chess players.

Attentional Control:

The brain's ability to focus begins with attentional control, which allows us to selectively concentrate on specific stimuli while filtering out irrelevant information.

Magnus Carlsen and Vishwanathan Anand demonstrate exceptional attentional control. They can zone in on the chessboard, analyzing positions and planning moves with laser-like precision, while ignoring distractions around them.

Working Memory:

Working memory is like the brain's mental workspace, where information is temporarily stored and manipulated to complete tasks.

Chess grandmasters like Garry Kasparov and Judit Polgar possess remarkable working memory capacity. They can hold multiple chess positions in their minds, visualize future moves, and anticipate their opponents' strategies, all while maintaining focus on the game at hand.

Inhibition:

Inhibition is the brain's ability to suppress irrelevant or distracting thoughts, impulses, or behaviors.

Top chess players, such as Bobby Fischer and Hou Yifan, demonstrate exceptional inhibition skills. They can block out external distractions, silence self-doubt, and maintain unwavering focus on the chessboard, even under pressure-filled tournament conditions.

Cognitive Flexibility:

Cognitive flexibility refers to the brain's capacity to adapt and switch between different tasks or mental states.

Chess champions like Anatoly Karpov and Hou Yifan exhibit remarkable cognitive flexibility. They can shift between different strategies, adjust their game plan on the fly, and quickly adapt to changing circumstances, all while staying fully engaged in the game.

So, the brain's ability to process focus involves a complex interplay of attentional control, working memory, inhibition, and cognitive flexibility. By studying the cognitive mechanisms at play in world-class chess players, we can gain valuable insights into how to enhance our own focus and concentration in various aspects of life. Whether we're tackling a challenging project at work, studying for an exam, or pursuing a personal goal, understanding how the brain processes focus can help us sharpen our mental skills and achieve greater success.

To understand how the brain processes focus, let's take a peek inside this remarkable organ. At the heart of our ability to focus is a network of interconnected regions in the brain, collectively known as the attentional system. This system includes areas such as the prefrontal cortex, which governs executive functions like decision-making and problem-solving, and the parietal cortex, which helps us orient our attention to relevant stimuli in our environment.

When we engage in a task that requires focus, such as reading a book or solving a puzzle, these regions of the brain spring into action. Neurons fire and form neural circuits, creating pathways that facilitate the processing of information related to the task at hand. As a result, our attention becomes selectively directed towards the relevant stimuli, while irrelevant distractions are filtered out.

But the process of focus is not solely determined by the brain's internal mechanisms – external factors also play a significant role. Environmental cues, such as noise, visual stimuli, and even social interactions, can either enhance or disrupt our ability to focus. For example, a noisy workplace may make it challenging to concentrate on a complex task, while a quiet, well-lit room may promote optimal focus.

The science of focus is a fascinating field that sheds light on how the brain processes information and directs attention. By understanding the neural mechanisms underlying focus and learning, we can cultivate our own ability to concentrate, block out distractions, and achieve peak performance in whatever endeavors we pursue.

Factors Influencing Concentration

Concentration is like a delicate thread that weaves through the fabric of our thoughts, holding our attention steady in the face of distractions. Yet, maintaining focus is no easy feat, requiring a delicate balance of internal and external factors. Let's explore some of the key elements that influence our ability to concentrate, drawing inspiration from the experiences of world-class chess players.

Passion and Purpose: Consider the story of Magnus Carlsen, widely regarded as one of the greatest chess players of all time. From a young age, Magnus displayed an insatiable passion for the game, spending hours poring over chess books and honing his skills. His unwavering dedication to chess fueled his concentration, allowing him to immerse himself fully in the complexities of the game. Similarly, when we are passionate about our pursuits and driven by a sense of purpose, our concentration naturally deepens, enabling us to stay focused and engaged even in the face of challenges.

Mindfulness and Presence: In this era of competitive chess, every move counts, requiring players to remain fully present and attentive to the unfolding dynamics of the game. Take the example of Judit Polgár, the strongest female chess player in history. Known for her exceptional ability to stay focused under pressure, Judit cultivated mindfulness and presence as essential tools in her arsenal. By staying rooted in the present moment and maintaining a clear awareness of her surroundings, she was able to tune out distractions and make strategic decisions with clarity and precision.

Mental Discipline and Resilience: Chess is a game of mental fortitude, demanding unwavering discipline and resilience in the face of adversity. Consider the remarkable journey of Vishwanathan Anand, the former World Chess Champion. Throughout his illustrious career, Anand faced numerous setbacks and challenges, yet he never wavered in his commitment to excellence. By cultivating mental discipline and resilience, Anand was able to weather the storms of competition and maintain his concentration even in the most intense moments of play. Similarly, when we cultivate inner strength and resilience, we enhance our capacity to sustain focus and overcome obstacles on our path.

Environment and External Factors: Our surroundings play a crucial role in shaping our ability to concentrate. Take the example of Bobby Fischer, whose legendary matches against Boris Spassky captured the world's attention. Fischer famously demanded optimal conditions for concentration, insisting on quiet, controlled environments free from distractions. By creating a conducive environment for focus, Fischer was able to channel his energies fully into the game, unleashing his formidable talent on the chessboard. Likewise, when we eliminate distractions and create a supportive environment for concentration, we set ourselves up for success in our endeavors.

Finally, concentration is a multifaceted skill influenced by numerous factors, from passion and purpose to mindfulness and mental resilience. By drawing inspiration from the experiences of world-class chess players, we can garner valuable insights into the art and science of concentration, empowering us to sharpen our focus and unlock our full potential in any endeavor we pursue.

Concentration, or the ability to focus our attention on a particular task or objective, is influenced by a variety of factors, both internal and external. Let's explore some of these factors and how they impact our ability to concentrate.

Environment: Our surroundings play a significant role in determining our level of concentration. A quiet, well-lit workspace devoid of distractions can enhance focus, while a noisy or cluttered environment may disrupt our ability to concentrate.

Mental State: Our mental and emotional state can also affect our concentration. Stress, anxiety, and fatigue can all impair our ability to focus, while feelings of calmness and positivity can enhance it.

Personal Motivation: The level of interest and motivation we have for a task can significantly impact our ability to concentrate. When we are passionate about what we're doing, we naturally find it easier to maintain focus and stay engaged.

Technology Use: In today's digital age, our constant connectivity to smartphones, social media, and other digital devices can pose a significant challenge to our ability to concentrate. The constant influx of notifications and distractions can make it difficult to maintain focus on important tasks.

Sleep and Nutrition: Our physical health also plays a crucial role in our ability to concentrate. Adequate sleep, regular exercise, and a balanced diet are essential for maintaining optimal cognitive function.

Concentration is influenced by a variety of factors, including our environment, mental state, personal motivation, technology use, and physical health. By understanding and addressing these factors, we can enhance our ability to focus and achieve greater success in our endeavors.

Crafting Crystal-Clear Goals

Setting clear goals is like charting a course for your journey in life. Just as a captain plots a course before setting sail, having well-defined goals provides direction and purpose, guiding you towards your desired destination. When you set clear goals, you establish a roadmap for success, outlining what you want to achieve and how you plan to get there.

Importance of Goal Setting in Enhancing Focus:

Goal setting plays a crucial role in enhancing focus by providing a clear target to aim for. When you have a specific goal in mind, your attention becomes naturally drawn towards it, helping you filter out distractions and stay on track. Let's explore the importance of goal setting in enhancing focus through the stories of some current famous individuals:

Setting goals is like drawing a map for your journey in life. It gives you direction, purpose, and a clear destination to strive towards. Now, let's dive into the world of chess, where goal setting plays a crucial role in enhancing focus and achieving success.

Imagine a young chess player, just starting out on their journey, dreams of becoming a grandmaster someday. They set their sights on this lofty goal and begin to chart their path forward. With each game they play, they focus not only on winning but also on improving their skills and strategy, inching closer to their ultimate objective.

Take the story of Magnus Carlsen, the former World Chess Champion. From a young age, Carlsen set his sights on mastering the game of chess and reaching the pinnacle of success. Through unwavering dedication and a relentless pursuit of excellence, he honed his skills and rose through the ranks to become one of the greatest chess players of all time.

But goal setting isn't just about achieving external success; it's also about personal growth and fulfillment. Consider the story of Judit Polgar, from a young age, Polgar set ambitious goals for herself, aiming to compete with and defeat the best players in the world, regardless of their gender. Through sheer determination and a laser-like focus on her goals, she shattered stereotypes and paved the way for future generations of female chess players.

These stories remind us of the power of goal setting in enhancing focus. When we have clear goals to strive towards, we become more disciplined, motivated, and resilient in the face of challenges. Our focus becomes laser-sharp as we channel our energy towards achieving our objectives, overcoming obstacles with determination and grace.

So, whether you're aiming to become a chess grandmaster, pursue a career goal, or embark on a personal journey of self-discovery, think about the importance of goal setting in enhancing focus. Set your goals high, stay committed to your vision, and let your unwavering focus propel you towards success and fulfillment in all areas of life.

Techniques for Establishing SMART Goals:

SMART goals provide a structured framework for goal-setting that increases the likelihood of success. Let's explore some techniques for establishing SMART goals:

Setting goals is the first step towards turning the invisible into the visible. But not all goals are created equal. To ensure that our goals are achievable and meaningful, it's important to follow the SMART framework

– Specific, Measurable, Achievable, Relevant, and Time-bound. Let's explore each element of SMART goals through the inspiring stories of world-class chess players.

Specific:

Just like a chess player visualizes their next move, it's essential to be specific about our goals. Take the example of Magnus Carlsen, the former World Chess Champion. Magnus didn't just aim to become a better chess player; he set a specific goal to reach a certain Elo rating – a measure of a player's skill level in chess. By setting a clear and specific target, Magnus was able to focus his efforts and track his progress with precision.

Measurable:

In chess, every move is measurable – it's either a success or a setback. Similarly, our goals should be measurable to gauge our progress. Consider the story of Judit Polgar, the strongest female chess player in history. Judit didn't simply aspire to "improve" her game; she set measurable goals to reach specific Elo ratings and win prestigious tournaments. By quantifying her objectives, Judit could track her improvement over time and adjust her strategies accordingly.

Achievable:

While aiming high is admirable, it's essential to set goals that are realistically attainable. Look at the story of Bobby Fischer, a chess prodigy who became the youngest Grandmaster in history at that time. Fischer didn't start by aiming for the world championship; he set achievable goals to master the fundamentals of chess and win local tournaments. By setting incremental and attainable goals, Fischer laid the groundwork for his eventual ascent to greatness.

Relevant:

Just as each move in chess must contribute to the overall strategy, our goals should align with our values and aspirations. Take the example of Garry Kasparov, widely regarded as one of the greatest chess players of all time. Kasparov didn't pursue goals that were merely popular or lucrative; he focused on challenges that aligned with his passion for the game and his desire to push the boundaries of human achievement. By staying true to his values, Kasparov remained motivated and fulfilled throughout his career.

Time-bound:

In chess, time is of the essence – every move is made within a finite timeframe. Similarly, our goals should have clear deadlines to keep us focused and motivated. Consider the story of any Chess Grand Master. They don't leave their goals open-ended; they set deadlines to achieve specific milestones, such as winning tournaments or mastering new openings. By imposing time constraints, they create a sense of urgency that propelled them towards success.

By applying the principles of SMART goals and drawing inspiration from the strategic prowess of world-class chess players, we can set ourselves up for success in any endeavor. So let's be specific, measurable, achievable, relevant, and time-bound in our goal-setting, and watch as we make our dreams a reality, one move at a time.

Distraction-Free Living

Distractions are everywhere, nowadays. Whether it's the ping of a new email, the buzz of a notification on our phone, or the chatter of colleagues in the office, it's easy to lose focus amidst the constant noise. However, learning to identify and eliminate distractions is essential for achieving our goals and maximizing productivity. We'll explore common distractions and strategies for overcoming them, drawing inspiration from the world of chess.

Identifying Common Distractions:

Technology Temptations: One of the most prevalent distractions in today's digital age is technology. With smartphones, social media, and endless online content at our fingertips, it's all too easy to get sucked into a digital rabbit hole. Take the case of Magnus Carlsen, the former World Chess

Champion. Despite his mastery of the game, Carlsen admits to struggling with distractions during tournaments, particularly the allure of checking his phone for updates. To combat this, Carlsen employs a simple yet effective strategy – he leaves his phone in another room during games, eliminating the temptation altogether.

Environmental Interruptions: Another common source of distraction is our physical environment. Whether it's a noisy neighbor, a cluttered workspace, or constant interruptions from colleagues, environmental factors can derail our focus and productivity. Take the example of Viswanathan Anand, one of the greatest chess players of all time. In his early career, Anand faced numerous distractions during tournaments, from noisy spectators to uncomfortable playing conditions. Over time, Anand learned to block out external distractions by focusing solely on the chessboard in front of him, a skill that served him well throughout his illustrious career.

Mental Mindsets: Distractions aren't always external – they can also originate from within. Negative thoughts, self-doubt, and lack of focus can all sabotage our efforts to stay on task. Consider the case of Judit Polgar, the strongest female chess player in history. Despite facing skepticism and criticism from male competitors throughout her career, Polgar remained laser-focused on her goals, refusing to let external opinions distract her from her path to success. By cultivating a resilient mindset and staying true to her passion for chess, Polgar achieved remarkable feats on the chessboard, proving that inner strength is often the most potent weapon against distractions.

Time Steals: Finally, one of the sneakiest distractions of all is the thief of time. Procrastination, multitasking, and inefficient time management can all eat away at our productivity, leaving us feeling overwhelmed and unfocused. Despite his unparalleled talent on the chessboard, Fischer struggled with time management and discipline throughout his career, often procrastinating on important tasks and leaving things until the last minute. As a result, Fischer's potential was never fully realized, highlighting the importance of effective time management in overcoming distractions and achieving success.

Identifying and eliminating distractions is crucial for maintaining focus and achieving our goals. By learning from the experiences of chess champions like Magnus Carlsen, Viswanathan Anand, Judit Polgar, and Bobby Fischer, we can develop strategies to overcome common distractions and unlock our full potential in both chess and life.

Strategies for Minimizing Distraction

In professional chess, where every move can determine the outcome of a match, the ability to maintain focus is paramount. Grandmasters like Magnus Carlsen and Vishwanathan Anand have mastered the art of concentration, but they also face distractions that threaten to derail their game. Let's explore some strategies these chess legends use to minimize distractions and stay focused on the board.

Create a Distraction-Free Environment: In the lead-up to a tournament or match, players often seek out quiet, secluded spaces where they can immerse themselves in their preparation without interruption. Vishwanathan Anand, for example, famously retreated to a remote training camp in the mountains to focus solely on his game, free from the distractions of everyday life.

Set Clear Boundaries: Just as in chess, where boundaries delineate the playing field, setting clear boundaries in your environment can help minimize distractions. Magnus Carlsen is known for his disciplined approach to training, setting specific times for practice sessions and enforcing strict boundaries to prevent outside distractions from interfering with his focus.

Utilize Technology Wisely: While technology can be a source of distraction, it can also be a valuable tool for enhancing focus. Many chess players use specialized software and apps to analyze games, study openings, and improve their skills. By using technology effectively, players can optimize their training and minimize distractions.

Practice Mindfulness: Mindfulness techniques, such as meditation and deep breathing exercises, can help chess players maintain focus and stay present during games. Anatoly Karpov, a former world champion, often incorporates mindfulness practices into his training regimen, allowing him to remain calm and centered even in the midst of intense competition.

Develop Mental Resilience: In the unpredictable world of chess, where one wrong move can spell disaster, mental resilience is essential. Players must learn to bounce back from setbacks and stay focused on their long-term goals. Garry Kasparov, widely regarded as one of the greatest chess players of all time, illustrates this quality, overcoming numerous challenges throughout his career to achieve unparalleled success.

By implementing these strategies and drawing inspiration from the world of professional chess, we can all learn to minimize distractions and enhance our focus in pursuit of our goals, both on and off the board.

Enhancing Concentration Sharpness

Concentration is like a superpower that allows us to focus our attention on a single task or goal, blocking out distractions and enabling us to perform at our best. Whether it's studying for an exam, completing a work project, or engaging in a game of chess, sharpening our concentration can significantly enhance our performance and productivity.

Techniques for Improving Concentration:

Mindfulness Meditation: One powerful technique for improving concentration is mindfulness meditation. By practicing mindfulness, we learn to cultivate a present-moment awareness, training our minds to focus on the task at hand without getting caught up in distractions. Chess grandmasters like Magnus Carlsen are known to incorporate mindfulness practices into their training routines, helping them maintain peak concentration during intense matches.

Break Tasks into Smaller Steps: Breaking tasks into smaller, more manageable steps can also help improve concentration. Rather than feeling overwhelmed by the enormity of a task, breaking it down into smaller components allows us to focus on one step at a time, making progress gradually. Chess players often employ this strategy by focusing on individual moves or sequences rather than trying to anticipate the entire game's outcome at once.

Create a Distraction-Free Environment: Minimizing distractions in your environment is crucial for enhancing concentration. This may involve finding a quiet space to work or study, turning off notifications on your phone or computer, and establishing clear boundaries with others to prevent interruptions. Chess prodigy Bobby Fischer famously demanded complete silence during his matches, recognizing the importance of a distraction-free environment for maintaining focus.

Use Visualization Techniques: Visualization techniques can be powerful tools for improving concentration. By mentally rehearsing a task or visualizing yourself successfully completing it, you can prime your mind for focused action. Chess players often visualize different game scenarios and anticipate their opponents' moves, allowing them to stay several steps ahead and maintain concentration throughout the match.

Take Regular Breaks: Finally, taking regular breaks can help prevent mental fatigue and maintain concentration over an extended period. By allowing yourself short breaks between tasks or study sessions, you give your mind a chance to rest and recharge, improving overall focus and productivity. Chess champions like Garry Kasparov are known for taking strategic breaks during matches to refresh their minds and maintain peak concentration.

Incorporating these techniques into your daily routine can help you enhance your concentration and achieve greater success in whatever endeavors you pursue. Whether you're studying for exams, working on a project, or competing in a chess tournament, mastering the art of concentration can unlock new levels of performance and productivity. So, why not give these techniques a try and experience the transformative power of focused attention for yourself?

How to enhance concentration

Concentration is like a muscle – the more you exercise it, the stronger it becomes. Distractions are everywhere, making it challenging to maintain focus on the task at hand. However, with the right techniques and practice, we can enhance our concentration and improve our productivity and performance.

Exercises to Strengthen Focus:

Visualization Techniques: In the world of chess, visualization is a crucial skill. Grandmasters are known for their ability to mentally simulate moves and anticipate their opponent's strategies several moves ahead. To strengthen your focus, try practicing visualization exercises. Close your eyes and imagine yourself successfully completing a task or achieving a goal. Visualize the steps you need to take and the obstacles you may encounter along the way. By regularly engaging in visualization exercises, you can enhance your ability to stay focused and composed under pressure.

Meditation and Mindfulness: Chess players often rely on meditation and mindfulness techniques to sharpen their focus and clear their minds before a game. Just as in chess, where every move requires careful thought and consideration, meditation teaches us to observe our thoughts without judgment and gently redirect our attention back to the present moment. Take a few minutes each day to sit quietly and focus on your breath or a specific object. Notice when your mind starts to wander and gently bring it back to the present. Over time, you'll find that your ability to concentrate improves, both on and off the chessboard.

Deep Work Sessions: In chess, players often engage in what's known as "deep work" – uninterrupted periods of intense focus and concentration. Set aside dedicated blocks of time for deep work, during which you commit to working on a single task with full concentration. Minimize distractions by turning off notifications and finding a quiet, comfortable space to work. By immersing yourself fully in the task at hand, you'll train your brain to sustain focus for longer periods, ultimately improving your productivity and efficiency.

Physical Exercise: Physical fitness plays a crucial role in mental performance, and many chess players incorporate regular exercise into their routines to maintain peak cognitive function. Engage in activities that get your heart pumping and your blood flowing, such as running, swimming, or cycling. Not only does exercise improve overall brain health, but it also reduces stress and boosts mood, making it easier to maintain focus and concentration.

Breaks and Rest: Finally, think about the importance of taking regular breaks and allowing yourself time to rest and recharge. Just as chess players strategically pace themselves throughout a game, balancing periods of intense focus with moments of relaxation and reflection, you too should prioritize self-care. Step away from your work or studies periodically, go for a walk, or engage in a hobby you enjoy. By giving your mind a chance to rest, you'll return to your tasks feeling refreshed and ready to tackle challenges with renewed focus and energy.

Enhancing concentration is a skill that can be developed through practice and perseverance. By incorporating visualization techniques, meditation, deep work sessions, physical exercise, and breaks into your routine, you can strengthen your focus and improve your ability to stay engaged and productive in any endeavor. Just like the chess masters who carefully hone their skills through dedicated practice, you too can train your mind to achieve greater levels of concentration and success.

Incorporating Mindfulness Practices

Imagine a chess grandmaster, sitting at the board with unwavering focus, contemplating each move with precision and clarity. Despite the high stakes of the game and the pressure of the competition, the grandmaster remains calm and composed, his mind attuned to the present moment.

Mindfulness has become a valuable tool for players seeking to sharpen their focus and enhance their performance. By incorporating mindfulness practices into their training regimen, chess players are discovering new ways to cultivate mental clarity, manage stress, and harness the power of their minds.

Magnus Carlsen is known for his exceptional strategic prowess and calm demeanor at the board. Carlsen has spoken openly about the role of mindfulness in his preparation and performance, crediting meditation as a key component of his success.

For Carlsen, mindfulness is not just about staying focused during games; it's about cultivating a deeper awareness of his thoughts, emotions, and reactions both on and off the chessboard. By practicing mindfulness meditation regularly, Carlsen has learned to observe his mind with greater clarity, allowing him to make more deliberate decisions and maintain a sense of calm under pressure.

Similarly, other top chess players, such as Viswanathan Anand and Hou Yifan, have embraced mindfulness as a way to enhance their mental resilience and improve their overall well-being. Through practices like meditation, deep breathing exercises, and visualization techniques, these players have found ways to quiet their minds, reduce anxiety, and enter a state of flow where their performance peaks.

But mindfulness isn't just for elite players; it's a practice that anyone can incorporate into their daily lives to reap its benefits. Whether you're a seasoned chess player or a beginner just starting out, mindfulness can help you stay grounded, focused, and present in the moment, both on and off the board.

By integrating mindfulness practices into your chess training routine, you can cultivate greater awareness, sharpen your concentration, and unlock new levels of performance. So, the next time you sit down to play a game of chess, take a moment to center yourself, connect with your breath, and embrace the power of mindfulness to guide you towards victory.

Mindfulness and Meditation have become buzzwords in recent years, but their roots go back thousands of years, originating from ancient practices in various cultures. One of the key benefits of meditation is its ability to enhance focus and concentration. Let's explore how meditation has made a significant impact on individuals, including some notable figures in the world of chess.

Benefits of Meditation for Focus:

Enhanced Concentration: Meditation helps train the mind to focus on the present moment, leading to improved concentration. In the world of chess, where strategic thinking and intense focus are paramount, meditation can be a game-changer. Take the example of Vidit Gujarati, one of the top Grand Master in the World of Chess. Vidit attributes his success partly to his meditation practice, which allows him to maintain a clear and focused mind during high-pressure matches.

Stress Reduction: Stress and anxiety can be major distractions that hinder focus. Meditation acts as a powerful antidote to stress, promoting relaxation and inner peace. For chess players like Garry Kasparov, the legendary grandmaster, meditation has been instrumental in managing the immense pressure of competitive play. By incorporating mindfulness techniques into his routine, Kasparov maintains a calm and composed demeanor, enabling him to make precise and strategic moves on the chessboard.

Improved Decision Making: Meditation cultivates awareness and clarity of thought, which are essential for making sound decisions. In chess, where every move carries weighty consequences, the ability to make optimal decisions is critical. Vishwanathan Anand, the former World Chess Champion, is known for his exceptional decision-making skills on the board. Anand attributes his mental clarity and sharp intuition to his regular meditation practice, which enhances his ability to assess positions and devise winning strategies.

Heightened Creativity: Meditation has been shown to stimulate creativity by quieting the mind and fostering a state of receptivity to new ideas. In chess, creativity is prized as players strive to devise innovative strategies and outmaneuver their opponents. Hikaru Nakamura, a top-ranked American chess grandmaster, incorporates mindfulness meditation into his training regimen to spark creative insights and breakthroughs in his gameplay.

Emotional Regulation: Emotional resilience is crucial in competitive settings, including chess tournaments. Meditation promotes emotional regulation by cultivating a sense of inner balance and equanimity. Fabiano Caruana, an American chess prodigy and former World Championship challenger, emphasizes the role of meditation in helping him maintain composure during intense matches. By staying emotionally grounded, Caruana is better able to navigate the ups and downs of competitive chess and sustain his focus for prolonged periods.

Meditation offers a myriad of benefits for enhancing focus, concentration, and mental acuity, making it a valuable tool for individuals seeking to excel in their endeavors, including the highly competitive world of chess. Through the stories of chess masters who have integrated meditation into their training routines, we gain insight into the profound impact of mindfulness practices on cognitive performance and strategic thinking. As we continue to explore the intersection of mindfulness and meditation with various domains of human endeavor, it becomes increasingly evident that cultivating a mindful awareness can unlock new levels of excellence and achievement.

Maximizing Efficiency and Output

Mastering the art of time management is essential for achieving productivity and success. Just like a chess player strategically plans each move to outsmart their opponent, effective time management involves making smart decisions about how to allocate our time to maximize productivity. Let's explore some techniques inspired by the world of chess that can help us manage our time more effectively.

Prioritize Like a Grandmaster:

In chess, grandmasters don't just move pieces randomly; they prioritize their moves based on the importance of each piece and the overall strategy of the game. Similarly, in time management, prioritizing tasks is crucial. Start by identifying the most important tasks – those that will have the biggest impact on your goals – and tackle them first. This ensures that you're making progress on the things that matter most.

Use the Pomodoro Technique:

The Pomodoro Technique is a time management method that involves breaking your work into short, focused intervals (usually 25 minutes) followed by a brief break. This technique mirrors the way chess players approach the game, with each move requiring intense focus and concentration. By working in short bursts and taking regular breaks, you can maintain high levels of productivity and avoid burnout.

Delegate Like a Chess Coach:

In the world of chess, coaches delegate tasks to their players based on their strengths and weaknesses. Similarly, in time management, delegating tasks to others can help lighten your workload and free up time for more important activities. Identify tasks that can be outsourced or delegated to colleagues or team members, allowing you to focus on higher-priority tasks that require your expertise.

Plan Your Day Like a Chess Opening:

Just as chess players study opening moves to gain an advantage in the game, planning your day in advance can give you a head start on productivity. Take a few minutes each morning to outline your tasks and goals for the day, considering how each task fits into your overall strategy. This proactive approach sets the tone for a productive day and helps you stay focused on what matters most.

Practice Time Blocking:

Time blocking involves scheduling specific blocks of time for different tasks or activities. This technique is similar to how chess players allocate time for each move, ensuring they stay within the game's time limits. By allocating dedicated time slots for tasks such as emails, meetings, and focused work, you can maintain a structured approach to your day and avoid distractions.

Real Stories from the Chess World:

Bobby Fischer's Legendary Focus:

Bobby Fischer, one of the greatest chess players of all time, was known for his legendary focus and concentration during games. He would often spend hours studying chess positions and practicing tactics, honing his skills to perfection. Fischer's dedication to his craft serves as a powerful reminder of the importance of focus and discipline in achieving success.

Garry Kasparov's Strategic Thinking:

Garry Kasparov, another chess legend, was renowned for his strategic thinking and ability to outmaneuver opponents. He approached each game with a carefully crafted plan, anticipating his opponent's moves and adjusting his strategy accordingly. Kasparov's strategic approach to chess illustrates the value of planning and foresight in achieving victory – lessons that apply equally to effective time management.

Judit Polgar's Time Management:

Judit Polgar, the strongest female chess player in history, excelled not only in her playing skills but also in her time management abilities. Despite competing against opponents with more experience and resources, Polgar leveraged her time effectively, focusing on continuous improvement and strategic play. Her success demonstrates the power of efficient time management in overcoming obstacles and achieving one's goals.

Just like a chess player carefully plans each move to outwit their opponent, you too can strategize and prioritize to accomplish your goals and maximize your potential.

Time management & Focus

Time management and productivity go hand in hand, like pieces on a chessboard working in harmony to achieve victory. But what if I told you that the key to mastering time management lies not just in juggling tasks, but in aligning it with focus? Let's explore this concept through the lens of the chess world, where every move counts and strategic thinking reigns supreme.

In the realm of chess, time management is critical. Players are allotted a set amount of time to make their moves, and every second spent pondering a move is precious. Take, for example, the legendary chess grandmaster Bobby Fischer. Known for his exceptional time management skills, Fischer would often spend hours analyzing potential moves in his head before making a decisive play. His ability to focus his time and energy on the most critical aspects of the game allowed him to outmaneuver his opponents and secure victory after victory.

Similarly, in our daily lives, aligning time management with focus can significantly impact our productivity. Just as Fischer meticulously planned his moves on the chessboard, we too can strategize our time to maximize efficiency and achieve our goals. By prioritizing tasks based on their importance and dedicating focused blocks of time to tackle them, we can work smarter, not harder.

Consider the story of Magnus Carlsen, the current World Chess Champion. Known for his lightning-fast decision-making and unwavering focus, Carlsen embodies the principles of effective time management. In a game where every move is scrutinized and analyzed, Carlsen trusts his instincts and commits to his decisions with confidence.

He understands that time is a limited resource and allocates it wisely, allowing him to stay ahead of his opponents and maintain his competitive edge.

In our own lives, we can emulate Carlsen's approach by cultivating a mindset of decisive action and unwavering focus. Rather than succumbing to analysis paralysis or getting bogged down by indecision, we can trust our instincts and commit to our chosen course of action. By aligning our time management strategies with our ability to focus on the task at hand, we can increase our productivity and make meaningful progress towards our goals.

Therefore, mastering time management and productivity requires more than just a checklist of tasks – it demands a strategic alignment of our time and energy with our ability to focus. By drawing inspiration from the chess world and adopting the mindset of strategic thinkers like Bobby Fischer and

Magnus Carlsen, we can enhance our time management skills and achieve greater success in all areas of our lives. So, let's make every move count and play the game of life with intention, focus, and purpose.

Building Unbreakable Mental Strength

In competitive chess, mental resilience is as vital as strategic brilliance. Players face relentless pressure, intense concentration, and grueling hours of play, making mental fatigue and burnout common challenges. However, the stories of resilience and triumph in the chess world offer valuable lessons on overcoming these obstacles.

Carlsen's journey to the top of the chess world was not without its challenges. Despite his exceptional talent, he faced setbacks and periods of self-doubt. However, Carlsen's resilience shone through in his ability to bounce back from defeats, learn from his mistakes, and adapt his approach. His unwavering determination and mental toughness propelled him to become one of the greatest chess players of all time.

Another example is Garry Kasparov, widely regarded as one of the greatest chess players in history. Throughout his career, Kasparov faced numerous grueling battles on the chessboard, often enduring marathon matches that tested his endurance and mental fortitude. Yet, despite the immense pressure and scrutiny, Kasparov remained remarkably resilient, refusing to succumb to fatigue or burnout. His ability to stay focused and composed under pressure was a testament to his mental resilience and unwavering dedication to the game.

These stories highlight the importance of developing mental resilience to navigate the challenges of competitive chess and overcome mental fatigue and burnout. Here are some key strategies that chess players – and anyone facing demanding challenges – can employ to cultivate mental resilience:

Mindfulness and Relaxation Techniques: Incorporating mindfulness practices and relaxation techniques, such as deep breathing exercises and visualization, can help chess players manage stress and stay calm under pressure.

Setting Realistic Goals: Setting realistic and achievable goals allows players to focus their energy and attention on specific objectives, reducing the risk of burnout from trying to do too much at once.

Taking Breaks and Rest: Recognizing the signs of mental fatigue and knowing when to take breaks is crucial for maintaining mental resilience. Stepping away from the chessboard to recharge and rest can help players return with renewed focus and clarity.

Seeking Support and Guidance: Building a support network of coaches, mentors, and fellow players can provide invaluable encouragement and guidance during challenging times. Having someone to lean on and share experiences with can bolster mental resilience and offer fresh perspectives on overcoming obstacles.

Embracing Failure as Growth: Viewing setbacks and failures as opportunities for growth and learning is essential for building mental resilience. By reframing adversity as a stepping stone to success, chess players can bounce back stronger and more resilient than before.

By incorporating these strategies into their approach to the game, chess players can develop the mental resilience needed to overcome mental fatigue and burnout and continue striving for excellence on the chessboard.

Building Resilience for Sustained Focus

Developing mental resilience is crucial for maintaining sustained focus in the current environment. Just like a muscle that grows stronger with exercise, our ability to stay focused can be nurtured and fortified through deliberate practice and resilience-building strategies.

Magnus Carlsen became the World Chess Champion at the age of 22. Carlsen's journey to the top was marked by countless setbacks and challenges, but what set him apart was his unwavering mental resilience. In one memorable match against Russian grandmaster Sergey Karjakin, Carlsen found himself in a difficult position and on the brink of defeat. However, instead of succumbing to pressure, he remained calm and focused, ultimately turning the game around to secure victory. This ability to bounce back from adversity and maintain focus under pressure is a hallmark of mental resilience.

Similarly, Garry Kasparov, widely regarded as one of the greatest chess players of all time, exemplifies the importance of resilience in sustaining focus. Throughout his illustrious career, Kasparov faced formidable opponents and encountered numerous setbacks. Yet, he never allowed these challenges to derail his focus or dampen his determination. Instead, he embraced adversity as an opportunity for growth and continued to push himself to new heights of excellence.

So, to build resilience, it's essential to cultivate a growth mindset – a belief that challenges are opportunities for learning and improvement, rather than insurmountable obstacles. Additionally, practicing mindfulness and stress management techniques can help bolster our mental resilience and enhance our ability to stay focused in the face of adversity. Just as chess players learn to quiet their minds and block out distractions during intense matches, we too can benefit from mindfulness practices that cultivate present-moment awareness and inner calm.

Furthermore, seeking support from mentors and peers can provide invaluable encouragement and guidance on our journey to building mental resilience. Just as chess players rely on coaches and fellow players for feedback and support, we can turn to trusted individuals in our lives for encouragement and perspective during challenging times.

Building resilience for sustained focus is a lifelong journey that requires dedication, practice, and a willingness to embrace adversity as an opportunity for growth. By drawing inspiration from the stories of chess champions like Magnus Carlsen and Garry Kasparov, we can cultivate the mental resilience needed to stay focused, overcome challenges, and achieve our goals in any endeavor we pursue.

Designing Your Perfect Workspace

In chess, where mental prowess reigns supreme, creating an optimal work environment is essential for players to perform at their best. Let's delve into some real stories from the chess world to understand how the right environment can make all the difference.

Bobby Fischer's Loneliness: Legendary chess champion Bobby Fischer was known for his solitary approach to the game. He often retreated to isolated settings, away from distractions, to focus solely on his chess mastery. Fischer's preference for solitude highlights the importance of minimizing external disruptions and creating a quiet, focused atmosphere conducive to deep concentration.

The Fischer-Spassky Match: In the historic 1972 World Chess Championship match between Bobby Fischer and Boris Spassky, the environment played a crucial role in shaping the outcome. The match took place in Reykjavik, Iceland, where the serene surroundings and supportive atmosphere provided an ideal backdrop for the intense competition. The peaceful setting allowed the players to channel their energies into the game, free from the pressures of external distractions.

Garry Kasparov's Training Camps: Former World Chess Champion Garry Kasparov understood the significance of environment in honing his skills. He organized intensive training camps in remote locations, where he and fellow players immersed themselves in chess for days on end. These camps fostered friendship among players and created a focused, competitive atmosphere conducive to learning and improvement.

Magnus Carlsen's Team Dynamics: Former World Chess Champion Magnus Carlsen emphasizes the importance of teamwork and collaboration in his approach to chess. He surrounds himself with a team of skilled analysts, trainers, and advisors who support him in his quest for excellence. By cultivating a positive and supportive team environment, Carlsen maximizes his potential and stays motivated to push his limits.

The Impact of Technology: With the advent of online platforms and digital tools, chess players now have access to a wealth of resources for training and analysis. Grandmasters like Hikaru Nakamura and Wesley So harness the power of technology to simulate tournament conditions, analyze games, and collaborate with fellow players worldwide. This virtual environment offers flexibility and connectivity, enabling players to sharpen their skills and stay competitive in the ever-evolving world of chess.

Therefore, creating an optimal work environment in chess – or any endeavor – involves minimizing distractions, fostering collaboration, and leveraging resources effectively. Whether it's through solitude, supportive teams, or innovative technology, the right environment can empower us to achieve our goals and reach new heights of achievement.

Surrounding Yourself with Supportive Influences:

Support and mentorship play a vital role in a player's development and success in chess. Throughout his journey, Carlsen had the unwavering support of his family, particularly his father, Henrik Carlsen, who recognized his son's talent from a young age and nurtured his passion for the game.

Henrik Carlsen didn't just provide logistical support by driving Magnus to tournaments and arranging coaching sessions; he also offered emotional support and encouragement during the inevitable ups and downs of Magnus's chess career. This supportive environment allowed Magnus to focus on honing his skills and pursuing his dreams without being weighed down by doubt or negativity.

Similarly, in the case of American chess prodigy Bobby Fischer, who became the World Chess Champion in 1972, supportive influences played a critical role in his rise to the top. Fischer had a close-knit circle of mentors and advisors who recognized his extraordinary talent and provided guidance and support as he navigated the competitive world of chess.

One notable mentor in Fischer's life was Grandmaster William Lombardy, who served as Fischer's coach and confidant during his formative years. Lombardy not only helped Fischer refine his chess skills but also provided emotional support and stability during challenging times. With Lombardy's guidance, Fischer was able to focus on his game and achieve remarkable success on the international stage.

These stories illustrate the importance of surrounding ourselves with supportive influences. Whether it's family members, friends, mentors, or coaches, having a supportive network can make all the difference in our journey towards success. These individuals uplift us during difficult moments, celebrate our victories, and provide valuable insights and guidance that propel us forward.

In our own lives, we can cultivate a positive environment by seeking out supportive influences and nurturing those relationships. Whether it's joining a community of like-minded individuals, seeking mentorship from those who have walked the path before us, or simply surrounding ourselves with friends and family who believe in our potential, we have the power to shape our environment in a way that fosters growth, resilience, and positivity.

By prioritizing supportive influences and creating a nurturing environment, we set ourselves up for success and fulfillment in both our personal and professional endeavors. Just as Magnus Carlsen and Bobby Fischer thrived with the support of their mentors and loved ones, we too can achieve greatness when we surround ourselves with positivity and encouragement.

Strategies for Overcoming Common Obstacles

Life is a journey filled with challenges, obstacles, and setbacks. Each of us faces our fair share of difficulties along the way. However, it's how we respond to these challenges that ultimately determines our success and resilience.

Players often encounter obstacles that test their skills and determination. Let's explore some common challenges faced by chess players and the strategies they employ to overcome them.

Facing Tough Opponents:

One of the most common challenges in chess is facing opponents who are more skilled or experienced. Whether it's a seasoned grandmaster or a formidable rival at a local tournament, going up against tough competition can be daunting. However, instead of feeling intimidated, successful players approach these matchups as opportunities for growth and learning.

As a young prodigy, Carlsen faced off against seasoned veterans and top-ranked players, often with overwhelming odds against him. Despite the pressure, Carlsen remained undaunted, viewing each game as a chance to test his abilities and improve his skills. Through perseverance and determination, he steadily climbed the ranks and eventually became one of the greatest chess players of all time.

Strategy: To overcome the challenge of facing tough opponents, focus on playing your best game and learning from each experience. Analyze your games afterward to identify areas for improvement and adjust your strategy accordingly. Embrace the opportunity to challenge yourself and grow as a player, regardless of the outcome.

Dealing with Time Pressure:

Another common challenge in chess is managing time pressure during fast-paced games or tournaments. With the clock ticking down, players must make quick, decisive moves while maintaining accuracy and composure. For many players, the pressure of the clock can lead to mistakes and poor decisions.

Consider the case of Viswanathan Anand, a former World Chess Champion known for his exceptional speed and precision. In high-stakes games, Anand faced intense time pressure, with seconds ticking away as he deliberated over his moves. Yet, instead of succumbing to panic, Anand remained calm and focused, relying on his years of experience and instinct to guide him through challenging situations.

Strategy: To overcome time pressure, practice playing speed chess games and develop efficient decision-making skills. Prioritize your moves based on their importance and impact on the game, and avoid getting bogged down by indecision. Trust your instincts and stay focused on the objective, even when the clock is ticking.

Handling Mistakes and Losses:

In chess, as in life, mistakes and losses are inevitable. Whether it's overlooking a critical move or falling victim to a well-executed tactic, every player experiences setbacks on their journey. However, how we respond to these setbacks is what ultimately defines our growth and resilience as chess players and individuals.

Throughout his illustrious career, Kasparov faced numerous defeats and setbacks, including losses against formidable opponents and missed opportunities in critical games. However, instead of dwelling on his mistakes, Kasparov used them as learning opportunities, analyzing his games meticulously and adapting his strategy for future matches.

Strategy: To overcome mistakes and losses, adopt a growth mindset and view setbacks as opportunities for learning and improvement. Analyze your games objectively to identify areas for improvement and develop strategies to address them. Embrace the lessons learned from each experience and use them to fuel your growth and development as a player.

Finally, overcoming challenges in chess – and in life – requires resilience, determination, and a willingness to learn and adapt. By employing strategic thinking, maintaining composure under pressure, and embracing setbacks as opportunities for growth, players can overcome obstacles and achieve success on the chessboard and beyond.

Maintaining Focus During Adversity:

Maintaining focus during adversity is not just a skill – it's a necessity. In the 2018 World Chess Championship, Carlsen faced a formidable opponent in Fabiano Caruana. The tension was palpable as the two grandmasters engaged in a fierce battle of wits. However, amidst the pressure of the competition, Carlsen remained remarkably composed, exhibiting a level of focus that ultimately led to his victory.

One key strategy employed by Carlsen and other elite chess players is the ability to stay present in the moment, even when facing setbacks or challenges. In chess, every move matters, and a single mistake can change the course of the game. Despite this pressure, top players like Carlsen maintain their focus by focusing solely on the current position on the board, rather than dwelling on past errors or worrying about future outcomes.

Another example comes from the legendary Garry Kasparov, widely regarded as one of the greatest chess players of all time. In his historic match against IBM's Deep Blue computer in 1997, Kasparov found himself in a difficult position after losing the first game of the series. Many pundits predicted that he would crumble under the pressure, but Kasparov remained undeterred. Instead of allowing the setback to derail him, he doubled down on his focus and determination, ultimately winning the match and solidifying his status as a chess legend.

These stories from the world of chess offer valuable insights into the importance of maintaining focus during adversity. Whether facing a formidable opponent or navigating unexpected challenges, the ability to stay present, adapt to changing circumstances, and maintain clarity of thought is essential for success. By learning from the strategies employed by top chess players like Carlsen and Kasparov, we can cultivate our own resilience and focus, enabling us to overcome obstacles and achieve our goals, both on and off the chessboard.

Taking Control of Your Thoughts

The power of the mind reigns supreme in chess. Chess players must not only possess strategic prowess and tactical skill but also master the art of positive thinking to stay ahead of their opponents.

Positive thinking in chess isn't just about maintaining a sunny disposition; it's about cultivating a mindset that fosters resilience, creativity, and adaptability in the face of adversity. Let's explore how some of the greatest chess players in history have harnessed the power of positive thinking to achieve remarkable success on the board.

Anatoly Karpov, one of the most dominant players of his era, once said, "You must take your opponent into a deep dark forest where 2+2=5, and the path leading out is only wide enough for one." Karpov's words highlight the importance of maintaining a positive outlook even in the most challenging situations. By embracing the complexities of the game and viewing obstacles as opportunities for growth, Karpov was able to outmaneuver his opponents with grace and precision.

Another example of positive thinking in action can be found in the legendary Bobby Fischer. Despite facing formidable opponents and intense pressure, Fischer approached each game with unwavering confidence and belief in his abilities. His famous victory over Boris Spassky in the 1972 World Chess Championship demonstrated the power of positive thinking to overcome seemingly insurmountable odds and achieve greatness on the world stage.

In addition to individual brilliance, positive thinking also plays a crucial role in team dynamics, as evidenced by the success of the

Soviet chess team during the Cold War era. Despite facing political tensions and external pressures, Soviet players maintained a collective mindset focused on collaboration, camaraderie, and shared success. This positive team culture propelled them to numerous victories in international competitions and solidified their reputation as a dominant force in the chess world.

The stories of Karpov, Fischer, and the Soviet chess team underscore the transformative impact of positive thinking on performance and success. By cultivating a mindset rooted in optimism, resilience, and self-belief, chess players can overcome obstacles, adapt to challenges, and ultimately achieve their goals on and off the board.

Mastering your mind and harnessing the power of positive thinking are essential skills for success in chess and life. By adopting a positive mindset, embracing challenges as opportunities for growth, and believing in your abilities, you can unlock your full potential and achieve extraordinary results. So, the next time you sit down at the chessboard, follow the words of Karpov, Fischer, and countless other chess legends – positivity breeds success.

Cultivating a Growth Mindset

One of the key elements in achieving greatness in chess, and in life, is cultivating a growth mindset. This mindset is based on the belief that our abilities and intelligence can be developed through dedication and hard work, rather than being fixed traits that we're born with.

To understand the power of a growth mindset, let's take a look at the story of Magnus Carlsen, the former World Chess Champion. Carlsen's journey to the top of the chess world is a testament to the principles of growth mindset. Despite showing early promise in the game, Carlsen faced numerous setbacks and defeats along the way. However, instead of viewing these setbacks as failures, he saw them as opportunities for growth and learning. With each loss, Carlsen analyzed his mistakes, honed his skills, and emerged stronger and more resilient than before. His unwavering belief in his ability to improve propelled him to become one of the greatest chess players of all time.

Similarly, in our own lives, adopting a growth mindset can have a transformative impact. Instead of being discouraged by setbacks or challenges, we can view them as opportunities to learn and grow. Like pieces on a chessboard, our abilities may initially seem limited, but with dedication and practice, we can unlock our full potential and achieve remarkable success.

One of the hallmarks of a growth mindset is the willingness to embrace challenges. In chess, as in life, facing difficult opponents and complex positions is inevitable. Rather than shying away from these challenges, individuals with a growth mindset approach them with enthusiasm and curiosity. They see challenges as opportunities to stretch their abilities and push beyond their comfort zones, knowing that growth and improvement lie on the other side of adversity.

Take the story of Beth Harmon, the fictional protagonist of "The Queen's Gambit," for example. Despite facing numerous obstacles on her journey to becoming a chess prodigy, including personal struggles and societal barriers, Beth remained undeterred in her pursuit of excellence. With each setback, she persevered, learning from her mistakes and refining her skills. Through her unwavering determination and growth mindset, Beth ultimately rose to become a formidable force in the world of chess, inspiring countless others along the way.

In addition to embracing challenges, cultivating a growth mindset also involves embracing effort and persistence. In chess, as in life, success rarely comes easy. It requires dedication, practice, and a willingness to put in the hard work, even when faced with setbacks or slow progress. By adopting a mindset focused on continuous improvement and resilience, individuals can overcome obstacles and achieve their goals, both on and off the chessboard.

Finally, a growth mindset is characterized by a love of learning and a willingness to seek feedback. In chess, players are constantly analyzing games, studying opening theory, and seeking advice from coaches and peers to improve their skills. Similarly, in life, those with a growth mindset approach each day as an opportunity to learn something new and grow as individuals. They welcome feedback as a chance to gain insights and make improvements, knowing that the path to mastery is paved with continuous learning and self-reflection.

Mastering your mind and cultivating a growth mindset are essential ingredients for success in chess and in life. By embracing challenges, exerting effort, and maintaining a love of learning, individuals can unlock their full potential and achieve greatness. As Magnus Carlsen and Beth Harmon have demonstrated, with the right mindset, anything is possible – even conquering the seemingly unbeatable challenges that lie ahead.

The mindset of a person can make all the difference between success and failure. Arjun, another young chess Grand Master from India who dreamed of making a mark on the international stage. From a young age, Arjun displayed a natural talent for the game, but it was his mindset that truly set him apart.

Arjun understood the importance of cultivating a growth mindset – the belief that intelligence and abilities can be developed through dedication and hard work.

Arjun's journey to mastery was not without its obstacles. Like any aspiring chess player, he faced numerous setbacks and defeats along the way. But instead of being discouraged, Arjun saw each setback as a chance to learn and improve. He analyzed his games, identified areas for improvement, and relentlessly worked to refine his skills.

One of the most defining moments in Arjun's journey came during a particularly challenging tournament. Despite putting in hours of preparation, Arjun found himself struggling against formidable opponents. But rather than giving in to frustration, he remained focused and resilient, pushing himself to perform at his best with each move.

Arjun's perseverance paid off as he gradually climbed the ranks, earning recognition and accolades on both national and international platforms. His growth mindset drove him to success in World's top level chess.

By embracing challenges, persisting in the face of setbacks, and seeking opportunities for growth, we too can unlock our full potential and master our minds.

In our own lives, cultivating a growth mindset can open doors to new possibilities and empower us to overcome obstacles with resilience and determination. Whether we're pursuing our passions, chasing our dreams, or navigating the complexities of everyday life, adopting a growth mindset can lead to greater fulfillment, achievement, and personal growth.

So, let us follow in Arjun's footsteps and embrace the journey of self-discovery and improvement with a mindset fueled by curiosity, perseverance, and the belief that our potential knows no bounds. With a growth mindset as our guide, we can truly master our minds and unlock the limitless possibilities that lie within.

Final Thoughts

As we reach the end of our journey exploring the power of focus, it's time to reflect on the key insights we've gained along the way. Throughout this book, we've delved into the importance of focus and uncovered practical strategies for mastering this essential skill. Let's take a moment to summarize some of the key takeaways:

Summary of Key Insights:

Understanding the Nature of Focus: We've learned that focus is the ability to direct our attention and energy towards a specific task or goal. It involves tuning out distractions and maintaining concentration on what truly matters.

Recognizing the Benefits of Focus: By sharpening our focus, we can enhance our performance and productivity in various areas of life. Whether it's excelling in our careers, pursuing our passions, or fostering deeper connections with others, focus plays a crucial role in achieving our goals.

Cultivating Focus Through Practice: Just like any skill, focus can be developed and strengthened with practice. We've explored practical techniques such as mindfulness, time management, and goal setting, which can help us hone our ability to stay focused and engaged.

Overcoming Challenges and Distractions: Along our journey, we've encountered obstacles that threaten to derail our focus, from external distractions to internal doubts and fears. By adopting strategies such as prioritization, self-awareness, and resilience, we can navigate these challenges and stay on track towards our goals.

Embracing a Focus-Focused Mindset: Finally, we've explored the importance of cultivating a mindset that values focus and prioritizes it in our daily lives. By making intentional choices to protect our time and attention, we can create an environment that supports our focus and empowers us to thrive.

In closing, mastering the art of focus is not just about improving our productivity – it's about unlocking our full potential and living a more purposeful and fulfilling life. By applying the insights and techniques shared in this book, you have the power to cultivate a deeper sense of focus and achieve greater success and happiness in all that you do.

Please scan for the other book of the series
"Life Mastery".

Please scan the other book series, "The Art of Living"

www.ingramcontent.com/pod-product-compliance
Lightning Source LLC
Chambersburg PA
CBHW050118230526
45470CB00004B/1882